For David and Pam,
for disproving conventional wisdom about in-laws

The Little Book of Vicarage Wisdom

by
Catherine Fox

Illustrated by *Bridget Gillespie*

MONARCH
B O O K S

Mill Hill, London and Grand Rapids, Michigan

First published by Monarch Books in the UK in 2002,
Concorde House, Grenville Place, Mill Hill, London NW7 3SA.

Illustrations by Bridget Gillespie

Distributed by:
UK: STL, PO Box 300, Kingstown Broadway, Carlisle, Cumbria CA3 0QS;
USA: Kregel Publications, PO Box 2607, Grand Rapids, Michigan 49501.

ISBN 1 85424 603 8

Scripture quotations are taken from the Authorized Version of the Holy Bible,
King James Version, the rights of which are vested in the Crown's patentee,
Cambridge University Press.

British Library Cataloguing Data
A catalogue record for this book is available from the British Library.

Designed and produced for the publisher by
Gazelle Creative Productions,
Concorde House, Grenville Place, Mill Hill, London NW7 3SA.

Introduction

I put this Little Book humbly before the reader as a treasury of wisdom gleaned from my many years in the Vicarage. It is arranged in twelve inspirational sections to help you on your spiritual journey through the year. In a spirit of thrift, I offer you my very own budget proverbs – two for the price of one. Also included are those little hints on household matters which I know are always welcome. And lest the King James Bible slip from our race memory altogether, I am sharing with you my favourite scriptural proverbs in that version.

My thanks go to the many friends and relatives who have graciously or unwittingly allowed me to include their wisdom between the covers of this little volume. I pray that they will be given the grace always to bear in mind that plagiarism is the sincerest form of flattery.

Before you use this work as an aid to contemplation and the road to holistic spiritual tranquillity, a word of caution – if you place *The Little Book of Vicarage Wisdom* in your lavatory, it may disrupt the flow of chi round your U-bend.

Yours wisely from the Vicarage,
Catherine Fox

JANUARY

January brings the bills,
Tax demands and other ills.

It's an ill wind that butters no parsnips.

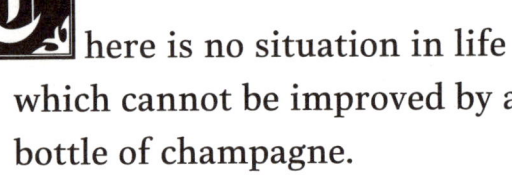 here is no situation in life which cannot be improved by a bottle of champagne.

If at first you don't succeed, tell yourself you didn't want to do it anyway.

An apple a day doesn't grow on trees.

"If Constable Eames would resist whistling 'Here we go gathering nuts in May'
I might resist putting him in the cell with this little lot."

If someone (or thing) is annoying you, why not make a soothing anagram out of their name?

Why not save a tree by ironing and re-using your Christmas wrapping paper?

hen in doubt, wear black.

*s the Good Book says*

"He that winketh with the eye causeth sorrow: but a prating fool shall fall." Proverbs 10:10a

 *seful Anagram*

Archbishop of Canterbury –
rhubarb confiscator hype

"They make wonderful forcing jars, dear."

FEBRUARY

February brings the overdraft
Pulled-in horns and increased
graft.

A fool and his money is a friend indeed.

Don't put all your eggs where your mouth is.

"Catherine Fox she may be but I detect no family resemblance."

You can never have too many feather boas.

"On the other hand..."

Nobody, however annoying, is a complete waste of carbon.

If you have two loaves, sell one and buy a Danish pastry.

Why not save a tree by re-using your pew sheet as a paper aeroplane?

*"I want to see Miss Biggles, the Sunday school teacher, **now**."*

You know you are getting old when the High Court judges start looking young.

seful Anagram

Archdeacon – acned roach

s the Good Book says

"Go to the ant, thou sluggard;
consider her ways, and be wise."
Proverbs 6:6

"Only a complete idiot would try mowing the lawn in this heat."

MARCH

March brings letters loud and shrill
From angry bankers out to kill.

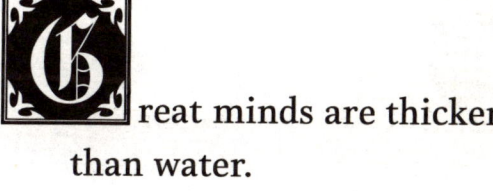reat minds are thicker than water.

leanliness does not pay.

on't stick dried peas up your nose.

All reactions are equally valid, but not all attract a custodial sentence.

If you find parallel parking stressful, try repeating this calming mantra to yourself: "That's what bumpers are for. That's what bumpers are for."

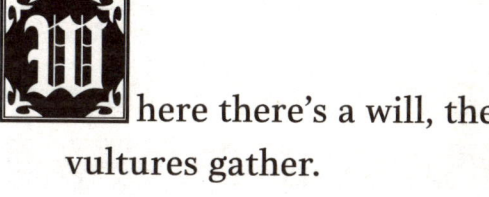here there's a will, the vultures gather.

Why not save a tree by re-using your paper aeroplanes as a low-calorie alternative to chewing gum?

"*Ah, Miss Biggles, always delighted to welcome another volunteer on to our cleaning rota.*"

*seful Anagram*

Rural dean – Laura Nerd

s the Good Book says

"The liberal soul shall be made fat: and he that watereth shall be watered also himself." Proverbs 11:25

APRIL

April brings the end of Lent
Now money is on chocolate spent.

Let sleeping dogs spoil the broth.

iscretion makes Jack a dull boy.

When you find yourself in a situation where every course of action is wrong from somebody's point of view, do what YOU want. That way at least one person will be happy.

You can say "no" to anything if you smile as you do it.

Don't pay for expensive salon waxing. Improvise at home with parcel tape.

Papier mâché for craft work can be made economically from chewed-up pew sheets.

"Mr Greese-Mordant won't like it, dearie.
He's always got 1st prize for his matchstick models of the church."

ife is too short for cleaning
wheelie bins.

Useful Anagram

Priest-in-charge – Easter chirping

s the Good Book says

"The slothful man roasteth not that which he took in hunting: but the substance of the diligent man is precious."

Proverbs 12:27

*"Swig of cider fer a bite of yer tossed organic chicken salsa
on wholewheat baguette, guv?"*

MAY

May is when the pinch is felt,
Time to tighten every belt.

e who hesitates gets the worm.

ools flock together.

You will always have enough to be generous.

Trying to take home that complimentary bottle of champagne *inside you* is a false economy.

Never run for buses while wearing hold-up stockings.

There is no disaster in life so embarrassing that it won't make a good anecdote afterwards. (See previous page.)

"Anyway, I just DIED of embarrassment."

You know you are grown up when you do what you want, even though other people want you to do it.

seful Anagram

Deanery Synod – reedy and nosy

*s the Good Book says*

"The hoary head is a crown of glory, if it be found in the way of righteousness."

Proverbs 16:31

JUNE

June brings rain and hail and sleet
Abandon thrift and comfort eat.

People who live in glass houses shouldn't skin a cat.

Drinking utensils vary in size. If you are faced with a large drink and do not know how many units of alcohol it contains, remember that the volume is proportional to the cube of the diameter. If you can calculate this, you are probably sober enough to drink it.

You can't have your cake
while the sun shines.

Try out an exotic new recipe. If you are having difficulty getting hold of expensive and unusual ingredients, why not move to a nicer area?

There is no such thing as weight gain, only clothes that have shrunk.

Remember, no act of kindness is ever wasted in a vicarage. Every cup of coffee served to an annoying parishioner may be offset against tax.

When official forms frustrate you, remember this calming tip:

If you write fast without removing your pen from the paper, block capitals can be made illegible.

 *seful Anagram*

Congregation – reacting goon

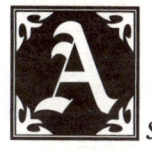*s the Good Book says*

"The glory of young men is
their strength: the beauty of old
men is the grey head."

Proverbs 20:29

JULY

Hot July brings summer sales
Restricted spending effort fails.

You can't make an omelette
out of a sow's ear.

bad penny is not gold.

Belgian chocolates are wasted on small children.

Help people to learn from their mistakes by always pointing them out.

"Mandy, can we go up a size to an 18 for cubicle 4 please?"

Children can be like bad hair days. Sometimes you wake up and you can't do a thing with them.

When you buy courgettes and other green vegetables, why not put them straight in the bin when you get home? This will save them from cluttering up the fridge for two weeks until they are mouldy.

Never be intimidated by goggle wearers at the swimming pool. Assert your right to swim widths and keep your hair dry.

seful Anagram

Sunday School – chaos soundly

s *the Good Book says*

"Be not among winebibbers:
among riotous eaters of flesh."
Proverbs 23:20

"If you'd listened to me, we'd be enjoying our usual two weeks in Jersey instead."

AUGUST

August, time to go abroad
To resorts you can't afford.

"I'm not quite sure the finances will stretch to Jersey this year."

t takes two to breed contempt.

"Sun, sand, sea. P.S. Don't forget, the dustmen come on Tuesdays."

eggars shouldn't throw stones.

When you are stressed, seek out the company of calm, wise people. There is always a chance you will wind them up, too.

Never get caught drunk in
charge of a pair of high heels.

others have rights too.

Admit to yourself you are never going to make a nourishing stock out of a chicken carcass.

ored with the sound of one hand clapping? Try imagining snails in slow motion instead.

The sun is always below the yardarm somewhere in the world.

*seful Anagram*

Church Commissioners –
comic richness humors

*s the Good Book says*

"Hast thou found honey? Eat so much as is sufficient for thee, lest thou be filled therewith, and vomit it." Proverbs 25:16

"Outside!"

SEPTEMBER

September, when schools
recommence
Now uniforms bring more
expense.

n apple a day killed the cat.

watched pot never won
fair lady.

It is more blessed to give than to receive. Never miss an opportunity to provide people with the chance to experience this blessing.

Don't be envious of young people's slenderness. Remind yourself that they are probably too neurotic to enjoy being thin.

There is no such thing as falling asleep during a sermon, only concentrating hard with your eyes closed and nodding occasionally in agreement.

Dusting is unhygienic. It puts asthma-inducing particles into the atmosphere for people to breathe.

Visit your library. A good novel is always better than TV.

seful Anagram

Flower rota – oral twofer

*s the Good Book says*

"As the door turneth upon his hinges, so doth the slothful upon his bed." Proverbs 26:14

OCTOBER

October when the clocks go back
Financial outlook seems more black.

No man is the mother of invention.

any hands keep the doctor away.

"Their union isn't going to be very happy when they realize he's not acting this one."

Don't do housework on the
Sabbath. It is the Day of Rest.

Every day is Sunday to the Christian.

Inside every thin person there is a fat person who has not eaten enough junk food.

ousework should only be done as a displacement activity.

ever floss your teeth
with someone else's hair.

"Why can't you use a proper toothpick like everyone else?"

s the Good Book says

"He that blesseth his friend with a loud voice, rising early in the morning, it shall be counted a curse to him." Proverbs 27:14

"Some folks just never learn."

seful Anagram

Lent Discussion Group –
Incredulous pigs' snot

NOVEMBER

November, buying gifts for folk
Despite the fact we're stony broke

It's no use crying over the camel's back.

The female of the species is more deadly than death and taxes.

ever accept ultimata from tradesmen.

Always concentrate when you are hoovering in the nude.

Don't fret if your small children ruin your lie-in. Patience is a virtue. You will be able to pay them back when they are teenagers.

"Come on Oliver – I'm sure your big cousin would love to join your band."

ron on a need-to-wear basis only.

"No dear, I DON'T thank God for the modern convenience of a cordless iron."

You know you are middle-aged when comfort takes precedence over vanity.

 seful Anagram

All-age Worship – Alas, gripe, howl

 s the Good Book says

"Surely the churning of milk bringeth forth butter, and the wringing of the nose bringeth forth blood: so the forcing of wrath bringeth forth strife." Proverbs 30:33

DECEMBER

December brings bills
by the score
To plunge us into debt
once more.

oo many cooks do what the Romans do.

"To our winners, a cheque and a fast getaway. To our losers…"

There's no smoke without breaking eggs.

Never attempt to clean your ears with a paperclip. Use a hairgrip like normal people.

Three intensely annoying things your children will say to you:

"Yeah, yeah, whatever."
"Why *me*?"
"Your point being?"

Three ways to embarrass your teenage children:

try to be cool,
dance at parties,
inhabit the same planet.

Don't bother dusting in December – just sprinkle glitter on the cobwebs.

*latitude for the Month*

It is better to seek the way
than weigh the Sikh.

*s the Good Book says*

"Even a fool, when he holdeth his peace is counted wise: and he that shutteth his lips is esteemed a man of understanding."

Proverbs 17:28

"I don't think it makes me look big, do you darling?"

seful Anagram

Altar frontal – floral tartan

And finally...

Never hang up on cold callers. It is discourteous. Instead, ask them if they have accepted Jesus as their personal Saviour, and *they* will hang up on *you*.

When writing a "To Do" list, always include one or two things you have already done, so that you can cross them off immediately.

Cheer up – you may not be suffering from low self esteem. It's possible that you only think you are because you are a pathetic deluded loser.

Never trust a surgeon who believes that the way to a man's heart is through his stomach.

ever wear white when eating curry.

Don't sneeze when you have just put a handful of peanuts into your mouth.

If you have read this book without a smile, you are clearly too wise to need it.